Zig Misiak: Author Jennifer Bettio: Illustrator

2022, ISBN 978-1-7771417-6-9

Other publications by Zig Misiak

FIRST NATIONS RESOURCE COLLECTION, ISBN 978-0-9811880-2-7

WAMPUM: The Story of Shaylyn the Clam, ISBN-978-0-9811880-8-9
WAR of 1812: Highlighting Native Nations, ISBN 978-0-9811880-5-8
WAR of 1812: Western Hooves of Thunder, ISBN 978-0-9811880-3-4
TONTO: The Man in Front of the Mask, ISBN 978-0-9811880-6-5

4 in 1 LEARNING: French & English, ISBN 978-0-9950128-0-6
ABC's Colouring Book, ISBN 978-0-9950128-9-9
1-2-3's, Shapes & Colours Colouring Book, ISBN 978-1-7771417-0-7
ASHER: of the Heron Clan, ISBN 978-0-9950128-3-7
COLTON: of the Bear Clan, ISBN 978-8-9950128-2-0
CRISTINE: of the Snipe Clan, ISBN 978-0-9950128-1-3
DARYL: of the Deer Clan, ISBN 978-0-9950128-6-8
ELLIE'S Butterfly Garden, ISBN 9781797484402
LUKE: of the Eel Clan, ISBN 978-0-9950128-8-2
MEAGHAN: of the Hawk Clan, ISBN 978-0-9950128-8-2
RYAN: of the Wolf Clan, ISBN 978-0-9950128-5-1
STANLEY: of the Beaver Clan, ISBN 978-0-9950128-8-2
TYLER: of the Turtle Clan, ISBN 978-0-9950128-1-3
POLISH Heritage Guide, ISBN 978-1-7771417-5-2
WALKER: In Grandpa's Food Garden, ISBN 978-1-7771417-6-9

www.canadianauthoreducation.com

Dedicated to
Walker Alexander Misiak
Our Grandson

Walker's Story

When Walker visited his grandpa and grandma's farm, he always ran toward the pond that was right beside the long driveway, leading to the house.

On the other side of the pond were two gardens. One was grandma's flower garden, that Walker's cousin Ellie liked, and the other was grandpas food garden that Walker enjoyed.

Both the flower garden and the food garden looked beautiful near the glistening, clear water of the pond that was surrounded by assorted bushes.

Grandpa always enjoyed being with Walker, teaching him how to create and take care of the food garden. Grandma and grandpa enjoyed the fresh vegetables all summer long and stored the rest of them to be eaten over the winter. During the summer months, they always gave fresh vegetables to Walker to take home."

Join Walker as he spends time helping grandpa and learning about all the plants that are grown in the garden.

They get planted together all in a row

One helps the other as they grow

The **corn** grows tall and the **beans** all around

The **squash** protects the roots near the ground

Corn, Beans and Squash
The 'Three Sisters' or 'Those that sustain us'.

Grandpa knelt near Walker's feet

We picked a bowl of berries for us to eat

They were not raspberries, blueberries nor cherries

But red, sun rip and juicy **strawberries**

Something that we pick in the fall

Is large, and shaped like a big ball

Most of them are orange and in the field they lie

Some made into Jack o' - lanterns others into **pumpkin** pie

“I like **potatoes** Grandpa. Where are they found?”

Grandpa replied, “They grow in rows under ground”.

Mashed, sliced, baked and French fries

“Did you know”, Grandpa said, “that potatoes have eyes?”

POTATOES

SPINACH

Many say that green vegetables are the best

Walker likes them too, but he also eats the rest

When Grandpa makes a tuna sandwich

He adds pepper, mayonnaise and leafs of **spinach**

Walker asked Grandpa if he liked muffins or cake

Grandpa answered, “My favorite is **carrot** to make and bake”

Rabbits love gardens and hop around to munch

I think that they like carrots to eat and crunch

CARROTS

Leafy, luscious and soft to the touch

Everyone likes **lettuce** ever so much

It is another vegetable that is good to grow

Planted in straight lines row after row

Plants can also be grown in a box.

Grandpa, Walker, and his big brother Colton.

They are round but do not grow underground like potatoes

Red and juicy, and my favorite, are **tomatoes**

Diced, sliced, chopped and many other uses

They are also squeezed to be made into juices

They come in different shapes and are mostly green

Cucumbers hide under leaves and hard to be seen

Pickled, chopped or sliced, thick or thinner

It is one of the things in a salad before dinner

KEY VOCABULARY

The Three Sisters are also referred to as 'Those that sustain us'.
Corn: It grows tall and straight. Corn originated in the Americas.
Beans: It will wrap around and grow up the corn stalk to get sunshine.
Squash: It will shade the roots from too much sun and hold in the moisture.

Asparagus: This vegetable originated in the Mediterranean.

Pumpkin: It is not a vegetable but a fruit. Its origins are in the Americas.

Potato: Peek-a-boo, potatoes have eyes. It is a root vegetable originating in the Americas.

Spinach: It originated from ancient Persia. It is referred to as a leafy vegetable.

Carrot: Carrots were first grown in Afghanistan. It is a root vegetable.

Lettuce: Originated in the Mediterranean area over 6000 years ago. It is a leafy vegetable.

Tomato: It is a fruit considered to be a vegetable. It originated in the Americas.

Cucumber: It is a fruit used as a vegetable. Originated in India.

****Definition of a fruit**: The botanical definition of fruit is a seed-bearing part of a flowering plant or tree that can be eaten as food.

FUN FACTS

There are more than 20,000 edible plants around the world.

Baby Carrots are not miniature carrots but full-sized carrots trimmed down in factories.

Beans, beans, are good for the heart, but the more you eat, the more you.......

Bell Peppers are often sold as 'Traffic Light Peppers'. Can you discover why?

Broccoli flowers are the part that we eat.

Brussel Sprouts are the world's most hated vegetable.

Carrots are almost 95% water.

Carrots can make your skin turn yellow for a while. Do you know why?

Corn is a member of the grass family.

Cucumbers are one of the vegetables you should not cook but always eat raw.

Spinach is good for you, as Popeye says, but not as good as many still believe.

Tomatoes are a fruit but considered a vegetable. Can you find out why?

Vegetables are grown from seeds.

Vegetable skins are full of nutrients and very good to eat.

Pumpkin patch colouring page

Zig Misiak is a highly respected, award-winning Canadian author of First Nations books and educational resources. He has received multiple awards, not all listed here, for his work and contributions, including two Governor-General's Awards.

Queen Elizabeth II Diamond Jubilee Medal
Queen Elizabeth II Platinum Award & Medal
Sovereign's Medal
Lieutenant Governor's Ontario Heritage Award for Lifetime Achievement
Polish Army Gold Medal - 1st Degree
Canadian Polish Congress Award of Merit
Polish Combatants' Bronze Cross
Shining Star Award
George and Olive Seibel Award
Inductee: Ancaster High School Hall of Distinction
Canadian Aboriginal Veterans Association Medallion
YMCA Peace Medal Nominee

As a child, often on his own, Zig became very curious about the children "across the bridge" from his house, at the nearby residential school in Brantford, Ontario. Then, as an adult, he embraced and cultivated interest and enduring relationships with his neighbours and friends, the Haudenosaunee, the Grand River Six Nations People.

Zig Misiak, became a well-known historical re-enactor who has travelled thousands of miles across Eastern Canada and the United States, participating in the re-enacting of major historical events from the French and Indian Wars, American Revolution, to the War of 1812. He also served in the Canadian Army, Royal Hamilton Light Infantry.

He is now recognized as an authority and a legend for his knowledge, understanding, and commitment to authenticity, as well as the strong friendships he has developed. He has studied and travelled to the very places he has written about in his many books. Zig has a deep love and respect for Indigenous People, recognizing that in spite of the many difficult challenges they have faced, they have remained true to their treaties. As Zig says, **"We must know them."**

Jennifer Bettio, of French-Canadian Métis background, born and raised in Guelph, Ontario, is an arts and photography graduate of Sheridan College. With the support of her parents, she pursued her interests in the arts field that has brought her great success. She does commissioned paintings, art, graphics and design, advertising, illustrations, and unique photography. She exhibits a unique First Nations and Métis style of art.

www.ingramcontent.com/pod-product-compliance
Lightning Source LLC
LaVergne TN
LVHW071133160826
845679LV00005B/1272
* 9 7 9 8 3 6 6 2 4 0 6 7 3 *